Motivation to
DESTINY
FULFILLMENT

Motivation to DESTINY FULFILLMENT

The Realities of Life

ELIOT MESSIAH

PARTRIDGE

To order additional copies of this book, contact
Toll Free 800 101 2657 (Singapore)
Toll Free 1 800 81 7340 (Malaysia)
orders.singapore@partridgepublishing.com

www.partridgepublishing.com/singapore

CONTENTS

ABSTRACT

The Destiny of man is more spiritual than physical. What ever happen in the physical is an outcome of what has already happened in the spirit. Destiny is part of human beings that would eventually happen in the future of which man has no control or power over. It is therefore beyond human effort. Herein, we looked at the fulfillment of destiny by looking at some biblical examples. We also considered the force behind man that pushes him to the fulfillment of his destiny; how could one be motivated to achieve that special destiny given him by the God of creation; and how the devil also tries to stop one from the fulfillment of his God given destiny. David was chosen by God as a man after His own heart. He was destined to rule over the people of Israel, but went

> *1 Samuel 13: 14*
> *......... the Lord has sought out (David) a man after His own heart, and the Lord has commanded him to be prince and ruler over His people, ... AMP*
>
> *Judges 16: 30*
> *And Samson cried; Let me die with the Philistine! And he bowed himself mightily, and the house fell upon the princes and upon all the people that were in it. ...... AMP*

through multiple challenges in the presence of King Saul. David eventually fulfilled his destiny to the fullest, because of his determination and reliance on God for strength and victory in all dimensions. Samson, in another hand died without fulfilling his full destiny by delivering his people (the Israelites) from the hand of their enemies (the Philistines), all because of the spiritual force of "lust after women" that he could not control. In Judges 16, you could see how Samson was tripped by Delilah and how he was disgraced before his death. It is therefore important to note that there are some unseen spirits that desire to destroy you and your destiny. Everyone has destiny and would be fulfilling that destiny in one way or the other.

Introduction

Everybody on this earth has a destiny to fulfill before the end of his time on earth. The destiny of life can be defined in so many ways, and according to the way each man sees and believes his destiny. Oxford Dictionary defines it to be *the events that will necessarily happen to a particular person in the future*. According to the Free Dictionary, *destiny is a predetermined course of event considered as something beyond human power or control*.

Just the way many are motivated in the organizational setting so as to achieve the best or put in the best to the fulfillment of the organizational goals and aims, destiny fulfillment in another hand is motivated by someone or something because of its need to be well fulfilled. Motivation in business setting can be said to be an influence either from internal or external on the employee so as to boost his moral to put in the best of his effort to the achievement of the organization's aims. The question that could be asked is that if an employee is motivated to putting in his best for the organization, then who motivates or influences the individual in achieving his destiny? Is it by someone outside or within, visible or invisible or by self-motivation? The quest to answer these questions would lead us to some Biblical truth.

Destiny fulfillment could be discussed from the academic point of view as well as religious view point. That notwithstanding, it is important to establish the fact that destiny is beyond human power and control. This therefore means that the discussion of destiny should be spiritually focused than academic knowledge and thinking. Hence, we can say that destiny fulfillment is beyond academic thinking. Let's now look at it in religious point of view by making reference to the BIBLE since we all can believe that the God of the Bible is the creator of man and hence, the destiny giver.

DESTINY

From the Bible, we could see that God has given destiny to everyone on earth, irrespective of the family one was born into or his/her religious background as well as that of his/her parents. We can identify from the Bible that there are two main categories of destiny that man is subject to fulfill during his earthly period, namely:

- **General destiny** *which is common to everyone and*
- **Specific destiny** *which is specific to the individual*

The destiny of a man is not given by parents or family members, neither is it determined by how rich or poor one's parents are or the circumstances surrounding one's birth, either through wanted or unwanted pregnancy, but from the "Almighty God" the giver of child and life. From the part of the world where I come from, a child's destiny can be foretold even when he is in the womb either by "babalawo – *worshiper of small gods*" or "Pastor – *worshiper of the Almighty God*". It means that the star of a child's destiny is released long before birth.

GENERAL DESTINY

This type of destiny is common to everyone on earth and it can be found in Genesis 1: 26-28. From the scripture, it was clear that after the creation of the universe, the following destinies were given to everyone on earth:

> *Genesis 1: 26-28*
> *……… So God created man in his own image, in the <u>image of God he created him</u>; male and female he created them. God blessed them and said to them, "<u>Be fruitful and increase in number; fill the earth and subdue it. Rule over</u> the fish of the sea and the birds of the air and over every living creature that moves on the ground." NIV*

I. To be in the image of God on earth no matter your religion

II. To have life

III. To have authority over the earth and rule over everything in it

IV. To be fruitful and increase in all aspect of life. This is the reason for reproduction, growth and increase in business

V. The fifth destiny of everyone is to work on the ground so as to earn a living as seen in Genesis 2:4-7

SPECIAL DESTINY

Everyone on earth, on individual basis has his/her personal destiny to fulfill, and this destiny is specific and unique to him/her alone. For example, a family could be with five children but their destinies would be different even if they are doing the same work or job, the approach they use on individual basis might not be the same as well as their interest.

> *1 Corinthians 2:7-9 "......... However, as it is written: 'No eye has seen, no ear has heard, no mind has conceived what God has prepared for those who love him'." NIV Reading scripture......Isaiah 64:4*

We can point out specifically that specific destiny or task has been allocated to everyone on individual ground and it is known to only him and the giver, "God". *In ["Jeremiah 1:4, 5" The word of the Lord came to me, saying "Before I formed you in the womb I knew you, before you were born I set you apart; I appointed you as a prophet to the nations."],* God told him (Jeremiah) before I formed you I knew you and have given you a task (destiny) which you must fulfill.

Isaiah says the Lord has called me from the womb: from the body of my mother He has named my name. In another word, we can say that our destiny names have been given us by God even before we were born. *[Isaiah 49:1, "Listen to me, O isles and coastlands, and hearken, you peoples from far. The Lord has called me from the womb; from the body of my mother He has named my name. "AMP]*

WHAT IS THEREFORE THAT SPECIFIC DESTINY OF MAN?

The specific destiny of man is that which he is born to do on earth within the periods of his living on earth. Anyone with no specific destiny has no reason whatsoever living on earth, less he becomes liability to others and society. In the same manner, anyone who finishes fulfilling his assigned destiny on earth has to give way for others and that is the reason for the existence of death.

From *Jeremiah 29:11 "For I know the plans I have for you, declares the LORD, "plans to prosper you and not to harm you, plans to give you hope and a future" we* can see that God has a specific plan and thought for everyone. The destiny of John the Baptist was to prepare the way for the coming of Jesus the Messiah by turning the heart of the people to their God, [Luke 1:11-17; Isaiah 40:3]. The work that Jesus came to do is the fulfillment of his destiny on earth, to show us the way to God and to die on the cross for the remission of our sins in order to reconcile us to the father (God), and that we might get back what the devil has **stolen** away from us.

The promise or the announcement of his birth says it all that ***"he will be great and will be called the Son of the Most High. The LORD God will give him the throne of his father David, and he will reign over the house of Jacob forever; and his kingdom will never end. Luke 1: 32-34".*** *Reading scripture……John 3:16, Matthew 26: 28*

The destiny of a man is therefore, that which he can do with <u>no much stress</u>, that which he find happiness in doing and that for which <u>outcome benefits others as well as the things of God</u>.

- <u>Not much stress</u> because whatever is of God, He has made way of fulfilling it and he goes all out to fulfill it. Therefore, for everything that involves the hand of God, stress cannot be there. Nevertheless, God has to allow you to go through certain things while doing them so that you do not lose focus as a result of too much ease.

  In another words, the things that we face as challenges in our way of destiny fulfillment are meant to keep us focus on God and trust him the more. They are to keep us in the timely plan of God; they are to remind us that it's not by our own effort but that of God so that we can give praise and testimony to the glory and honor of his name.

You don't give up when these challenges come, but press on the more because God has already make the way to success for you. He just wants to get your attention to himself at that time even though he already knew and has perfected the outcome. God is too loving and caring to have leaved you alone to challenges.

- <u>Outcome benefits others as well as the things of God</u>: This is because whatever destiny God commits to you is for the benefits of others and for Him (God) alone and that in doing them His name must and should be praised in them all. Any man using his destiny to benefit only himself and his family is on a selfish agenda and God would not be in it. This is because God is not a selfish God. The sun shines on everyone during the day; the moon gives light to everyone at night. God gives rain not only on the farm land of those who believe in his Son, but also to everyone so that the land may be fruitful to them all. God is not in a selfish business but rather a selfless business to save all and to give a fulfilled future to all so as to put happiness and joy into the face of all, to take us all from the captivity of poverty in every aspect of our lives. He is in the business of establishing us all to know him more.

It is however important to ask yourself the following questions in whatever it is that you do or that you dream to do, so as to know that specific destiny of yours:

- Do I have the desire to serve God as my Lord and savior in what I want to do?
- Would what I want to do give me happiness or do I find happiness in what I'm doing?
- Do I find fulfillment in what I am doing or would what I want to do give me fulfillment?
- Would it benefit others or in what ways could others benefit from what I do?

How to identify your destiny

From the few points identified so far, it is clear that destiny is a spiritual thing, and it's therefore controlled by a force in the spirit realm. Now that it is spiritual, then how can you know from the spirit what is it actually? Again, from the Bible,1 Corinthians 2:11, we know that it is only the spirit of man that can know his thought, likewise, it is only the spirit of God that can know the thought or the thinking of God. It therefore means that it's only the spirit that can know what is in the spirit. According to Romans 8:9, man is a spirit and can therefore know what is in his own spirit.

> *1 Corinthian 2:11*
> *"For who among men knows the thoughts of a man except the man's spirit within him? In the same way no one knows the thoughts of God except the Spirit of God." NIV*
>
> *Romans 8:9*
> *"You, however, are controlled not by the sinful nature but by the Spirit.............." NIV*

You can identify your destiny in the following ways:

- By asking God the giver of destiny through prayers to show you
- A man or woman of God can tell you your destiny by prophecy
- It can be identified through dreams, desires, aspirations as well as interest
- It can also be identified through what you like or don't like
- Devil, the falling angel can of course tell you your destiny as well

WHO CAN MOTIVATE YOU TO YOUR DESTINY?

Anyone can motivate you to achieve destiny in a positive or negative way. A teacher can motivate a student to destiny fulfillment, a pastor can motivate his church members to achieve destiny, a captain on a football field can motivate team members to winning and of course you can motivate yourself to a fulfilled destiny. Since we know that destiny is of the spirit, it's good to know also that <u>God can motivate his own</u> to fulfill destiny to their benefit and others while the <u>devil can also motivate his own</u> to fulfill destiny to their own destruction and the destruction of others. *[John 8:42-45 "Jesus said to them, "If God were your Father, you would love me, for I came from God and now am here. I have not come on my own; but he sent me. Why is my language not clear to you? <u>Because you are of your father, the devil,</u> and you want to carry out your father's desire. He was a murderer from the beginning, not holding to the truth, for there is no truth in him. When he lies, he*

speaks his native language, for he is a liar and the father of lies. Yet because I tell the truth, you do not believe me"], so whoever does not believe in Jesus or receive Him as Lord, is of the devil and the devil control such a person just like how God control those that believed in Him.

Let's now focus more on some of the spiritual influences or motivation to destiny fulfillment, since it has been noted that it's a thing beyond human control or power. And if it is beyond human control or power, then there is someone or a power in the spirit realm that controls it. Therefore, let's take a look at two main examples in the Bible to aid our understanding on the issue.

Genesis 37:2-11, at the age of eleven (11), Joseph began to see his destiny as a great man in the future and how he would be beneficial to

> *Genesis 37: 2-11*
> ...... *When his brothers saw that their father loved him more than any of them, they hated him and could not speak a kind word to him. Joseph had a dream, and when he told it to his brothers, they hated him all the more. He said to them,* "Listen to this dream I had; we were binding sheaves of grain out in the field when suddenly my sheaf rose and stood upright, while your sheaves gathered around mine and bowed down to it." *His brothers said to him, "Do you intend to reign over us? Will you actually rule us?" and they hated him all the more because of his dream and what he had said. Then he had another dream, and he told it to his brothers,* "Listen," *he said,* sun and moon and eleven stars were bowing down to me." *When he told his father as well as his brothers, his father rebuked him and said, "What is this dream you had? Will your mother and I and your brothers actually come and bow down to the ground before you?" his brothers were jealous of him, but his father kept the matter in mind. NIV*

others, but the devil didn't like it because he does not like anything good. Because of this, the devil put hatred into the heart of his brothers against him and his dream. In as much as the devil is working on destroying his dream, God was also busy working on the fulfillment of his dream because that is his special God given destiny. Instead of killing him, they sold him to slavery, even in slavery the devil still went after him just to kill him or to made him wrong his God by committing sin, but because he held unto God, he ended up in prison and even in prison, God was still with him motivating him about his dream for him to know that his dream is not dead. One most important thing that needs to be put across is that, while God is busy motivating you to fulfill destiny, the devil would also be busy trying to frustrate that same destiny, but if you are a child of God by accepting Jesus as your Lord and savior, your dream would surely come to fulfillment just at the time appointed by God. Look at this, when the time appointed for the dreams of Joseph to come to fulfillment came, God brought him out of the prison. My dear brothers and sisters, God knows the exact ways he would bring you out to establish the fulfillment of your destiny when the time appointed comes no matter how hard the devil get busy to destroy it. Joseph from prison became a prime minister in Egypt.

Moses was destined to lead the people of Israel to their land of promise from slavery in Egypt. But as it has earlier been identified that the destiny of a man is far known in the spirit before birth, the devil tried hard to destroy this destiny even before birth, in that the King of Egypt ordered the midwives to kill every male child at birth and when this did not work because of the fear of God in the heart of the midwives, another order was given to throw all the Hebrew male child to river Nile, Exodus 1: 15-22. However, God who is greater than the falling angel, Lucifer, and couldn't keep quiet for his promise to his people to be destroyed by the devil, turned everything on him (Pharaoh) so that Moses had to be trained in the house of the king of Egypt, Exodus 2: 5-10. All other effort of the devil to eliminate Moses before the time of his destiny fulfillment failed. Moses by the grace of God ran out of Egypt when he was identified not to be in support of the treatment given to the Hebrew people, but just like Joseph, when the time appointed came for the destiny of Moses (the promise of God to his people to be fulfilled), He brought back Moses to Egypt with his full backing.

Exodus 1: 15-22
The king of Egypt said to the Hebrew midwives, whose were Shiphrah and Puah, "When you help the Hebrew women in childbirth and observe them on the delivery stool, <u>if it is a boy, kill him; but if it is a girl, let her live.</u>" The midwives, however, feared God and did not do what the king of Egypt had told them to do; they let the boys live. .... Then Pharaoh gave this order to all his people: <u>"Every boy that is born you must throw into the Nile, but let every girl live.</u>" NIV

> *Exodus 2: 5-10*
> *Then Pharaoh's daughter went down to the Nile to bathe, and her attendants were walking along the river bank. She saw the basket among the reeds and sent her slave girl to get it. She opened it and saw the baby. He was crying, and she felt sorry for him. .... And the girl went and got the baby's mother. Pharaoh's daughter said to her, "<u>take this baby and nurse him for me, and I will pay you.</u>" So the woman took the baby and nursed him. When the child grew older, she took him to Pharaoh's daughter and he became her son. She named him Moses, saying, "I drew him out of the water." NIV*

My dear, the point I am trying to bring out to you here is that God would never leave you alone for your destiny to be destroyed by the devil, so long as you are His and willing to hold unto Him in fulfilling your dream to the glory of His name. The aim of the devil is to frustrate the specific destiny of man so that he would not be useful to himself and society, but rather a liability to society, while the aim of God for giving such particular destiny is to be useful to yourself and others around you. Note this point dear, *anything that you find interest in doing with happiness which praise God and benefit others you work with, but yet struggling to achieve a proper aim is actually your special destiny which the devil is busy trying to destroy by frustrating you to give up on it. If you hold unto it and call God into it, He would elevate you to glory just as it was for Joseph and Moses.*

From the biblical two examples among many, we can see that it is only God that can motivate man spiritually to fulfill destiny so as to be useful while the devil tries to frustrate you to waste your destiny and waste your life as well. Since the spiritual influence to destiny fulfillment is stronger, it is therefore good and advisable to know God and hold unto him at all times.

DESTINY FULFILLMENT

Every man on earth can only fulfill his/her destiny the way it is planned, designed and in the right time appointed if he gives his life to Jesus in totality. John 10:10, the devil comes just

> *John 10:10*
> *The thief comes only in order to steal and kill and destroy. I came that they may have and enjoy life, and have it in abundance (to the full, till it overflows). AMP*

to take away from you all the good things in your life so as to destroy you and kill you if he has the chance. The devil wanted to kill Joseph in order to kill his dream, and in the same way he tried to kill Moses, to kill the not yet fulfilled destiny at childbirth. But Jesus came to give life, hope, and future to motivate us to fulfill that glorious destiny even more abundantly and that is the good news to us.

One may ask, can devil give destiny to anyone and motivate him to fulfill it? Yes, he can by taking away from you the original one from God and replacing it with a fake one which he would motivate, supervise very well and see to it being fulfilled to the destruction of yourself and others, if care is not taking.

Dear, I would like you to note here that you can fulfill that which you have long "dreamed of becoming" if only you allow Jesus into the boat of your life. May be you are yet to fulfill destiny, then I would advise you to hold onto your God (Jesus) and ask of His motivation to the actual fulfillment of your dream of becoming that man or woman of influence to the glory of His name at the right time appointed. If by reading this book you think you have already missed it because what you are doing now is actually not what you have dreamt of and not finding the happiness you intend to in life, I have good news for you that **"it is not too late"**. It is God's doing that you see a new day so that you can recover by giving him a chance into your life and he would turn everything of the devil upside down and re-write them all for your good and happiness to the glory of His name. My dear, according to Revelation 3:20, if you can give Jesus a chance to hold the key to your heart, then you can smile again and remain in his love and you would find peace and enjoyment in whatever you do as a profession. Please, say the following prayers by faith and Jesus would be right ready to take over.

> *Revelation 3: 20*
> *Here I am! I stand at the door and knock. If anyone hears and my voice and opens the door, I will come in and eat with him, and he with me. NIV*

> *Lord Jesus, today I come before you because I understand that I need you in my life to fulfill my dreamed destiny. Forgive me my sins and cleanse me with your blood. Lord Jesus, the son of the most high God, take over my destiny and motivate me to fulfill it at the right time appointed to the glory of your name, in Jesus name I prayed, Amen!*

You are now a child of God, look for a Bible believing church if you don't have one and attend to grow your faith and hold unto Jesus at all times. Dear brethren, I wish you well in fulfilling your destiny (that which gives you happiness and bless others) to the praise of God.

PRESERVATION IN DESTINY PLAN

Now that you have dedicated or re-dedicated your life to Jesus to be the master and the motivator of your life to destiny fulfillment, you need to be preserved in him so that the destiny destroyer would not come back for your life.

The perfect way to fulfill your dreams, desires by becoming who you actually want to be is to fulfill them as a child of God. Just like how every child depends on his/her father for protection, support and counseling in whatever he/she desires, the same way you must also depend on God the father for support and protection. **"Those who live in the shelter of the Most High will find rest in the shadow of the Almighty"**. For us to rest in the shadow of the Almighty, which implies being under the protection of God, then we have to live (dwell) under His shelter. *How do we dwell under the shelter of God might be the question going through your mind.* The only way to dwell under His shelter is by putting all our trust on him, putting all hopes on him that with him we can become what we dreamt of. Living under the shelter of the Almighty is a total dependence on God that without Him I have no strength, without Him I am hopeless. It is interesting to know that all those who made it right are those with the mind that "I can't do it without God".

> Matthew 19:26 *"Jesus looked at them and said, "With man this is impossible, but with God all things are possible"." NIV*
> *Reading scriptures….. Matthew 7: 9-11 Romans 8: 28*

If we dwell under the shelter of the Almighty, all things shall be possible, our destiny fulfillment is assured with God.

> _Declaration:_ **Oh! LORD, because I love and trust in your name, rescue me and protect my destiny, protect my future, Oh! Lord. Answer me LORD when I call upon you and honor me and satisfy my soul with all good things you have destined for me in Jesus name.**

The destiny fulfillment of man is assured as long as he lives under the guidance, watch and control of the Almighty. Even though we trust in God for our destiny fulfillment, we have to wait upon Him because He is the only one with the perfect and right time appointed for the manifestation of our destiny.

Waiting on God

> *Habakkuk 2:3 "For the revelation awaits an appointed time;*
> *it speaks of the end and will not prove false. Though it linger,*
> *wait for it; it will certainly come and will not delay." NIV*
>
> *Genesis 18: 10-14 "then the LORD said, "I will surely return to*
> *you about this time next year, and Sarah your wife will have a*
> *son."…Is anything too hard for the LORD? I will return to you at*
> *the appointed time next year and Sarah will have a son." NIV*
>
> *Genesis 21: 1-3 "… Sarah became pregnant and*
> *bore a son to Abraham ….Abraham gave the name*
> *Isaac to the son Sarah bore him." NIV*

Waiting on the LORD for the appointed time is the best and perfect thing a child of God must do, because anything God gives to His children at the appointed time is the promise son (destiny) that would produce such fruit to bring the promise of peace and abundance to him. However, to many Christians, waiting on the LORD is the most difficult thing to do. What most people don't know is that doing it quick and having it fast is not what really matters, but doing it and having it right in God's time because that is the only way it can last and be enjoyed with happiness.

God is good, kind, truthful, loving and faithful to his promises. However, because He is God, He does things in His own appointed time and the time of God is what is good for his people, but unfortunately, waiting for God's time in realistic term is not easy, however, it's easy when living under his shelter and being guided by the Holy Spirit.

[Isaiah 40: 29-31 "He gives strength to the weary and increases the power of the weak. Even youths grow tired and weary, and young men stumble and fall; but those who hope in the LORD will renew their strength. They will soar on wings like eagles; they will run and not grow weary, they will walk and not be faint"]. Abraham was promised to be the father of all for many years, but he had not a son till he was old age and the wife was medically and humanly impossible to give birth. However, he held unto the promise and kept faithful to the things of God and it was counted to him as righteousness.

[Genesis 15: 5-7 "He took him outside and said, "Look up at the heavens and count the stars – if indeed you can count them." Then he said to him, "So shall your offspring be." Abram believed the LORD, and he credited it to him as righteousness. NIV]. Reading scripture….Romans 4:3

The LORD has given a promising future to each and every one to possess his/her possessions, but all these must happen within a specific time. Abraham waited on God faithfully and gave birth to the promise son, Isaac, at the right time.

Declaration: **Oh! LORD help me to wait on you, give me the grace to wait on your time to give birth to my promise Isaac because your time is the best for me and its only your time that is good for me. I will possess my possessions in and within the time of God in Jesus name. Amen!**

How to wait on God

The truth is that as we wait on God we get motivated and we also generate strength and hope to the fulfillment of our promising destiny. One can wait solely on God …

1. **The word of God:**

    > *John 1: 1-5 "In the beginning was the word, and the Word was with God. ………….". NIV*

    The word of God is referring to Jesus Christ. In the beginning was the word, which implies that, whenever we read the bible we are reading by looking on Jesus the Son of God. John 8: 31-32 **…that you shall know the truth and the truth shall set you free.** As we read the bible, we would identify the truth about our destiny. The truth of God is His purpose to His children. Studying and meditating on the word of God (the bible) gives us hope and faith to the fulfillment of our dreams. Because Jesus is the word of God, we get motivation from the word that makes us press on to fulfill our destiny even as the Holy Spirit gives us direction as to what to do and what not to do. The designs to the fulfillment of our dreams are all in the Bible which when discovered would motivate us to succeed.

2. **Keep faith:** Faith is an important tool to fulfillment in life. Faith keeps you in the hope of your dreams; it motivates you to keep pressing towards your dream and your ambitions. Why? Because there are times that it would seems as if you are not going to get there, at times it would be like your dream is dying, but with faith in the word of God, you can be assured that even if it takes time it would come perfectly with happiness, joy, peace, and inner refreshment. According to Paul the apostle, faith is the consideration of what you hope for and it gives assurance of what you did not yet seen. But I define faith in prayer as ....thanking God for what I have not yet seen or received... this is because by faith I know the promise of God, his perfect will shall surely come to pass in my life. It is important for us to know that God is not keeping us alive so as to disgrace us by frustrating our destiny plans and making us hopeless to be a laughing stock to others, but to give us a bright future, and honor us to the glory of His name.

Romans 10: 17, ***"Consequently, faith comes from hearing the message, and the message is heard through the word of Christ".*** *NIV.* The other thing we need to know is about how to put our faith to work. Having faith and sitting idle that it would work automatically is not the right type of faith, but the one that you work towards through prayer, and the word of God. You have a dream of becoming a medical doctor; that is your faith to a great future; but to what extent do you take your studies serious. God would bless on the actions you are taking towards your dream and favor you for elevation. There are times that people around you and seeing you working towards your faith might not believe that you can make it, because, they know your background, they know your parents and even your financial standing, but hey you don't need to give up but push on working toward it because God would always reward his faithful children with success. *If you doubt your faith because of what people say, because of what they do, because of the frustrations on the way making it as if it's impossible, then know that you don't have true faith but a doubtful faith and a doubtful faith would only result to fruitless efforts because God does not bless on such type of faith.*

3. **Fasting and Prayer:** Prayer is the life blood of every Christian. In order to fulfill the best of our dreams, we need to persist in prayer so as to keep the devil far away from us.

[1 Chronicles 4: 9-10 "Jabez was more honorable than his brothers. His mother had named him Jabez, saying, "I gave birth to him in pain." Jabez cried out to the God of Israel, "Oh that you would bless me and enlarge my territory! Let your hand be with me, and keep me from harm so that I will be free from pain." And God granted his request" NIV]. Jabez was destined to be successful and wealthy, but the devil who does not want anything good for us, prevented him from making it, however, Jabez prayed. The persistency of Jabez in knowing the truth that he is not supposed to be poor, to be begging and to be suffering, made him to press in prayer till God made him **more honorable**. It means therefore that the brothers also prayed but he prayed more than them. Jabez was more faithful in prayer than his brothers and as a result of his faithfulness and perseverance in prayer, the bible says: "and God granted his request". Sometimes, God has long before time released to us blessings, but the devil laid hands on them in one way or the other and we need to persist in fasting and prayer to have our destiny breakthrough.

4. **Keep away from sin:** In order not to give right to the devil to rob us of our blessings, we need to keep away from sin. You might ask what sin is. Anything that keeps you away from the presence of God is sin.

Anything that God frown his face against is sin. Sin is the only thing that can keep us away from God and hence given right to the devil to take our possessions from us. Holiness is therefore necessary.

Faithfulness and Truthfulness

In life, faithfulness and truthfulness are very important words that play essential role in one's life achievement. The earth is full of natural mineral resources like gold, oil and many more, in the same way man is also full of resource deposit. Just like how it takes a nation to identify those mineral resources, the same way it takes time for man to identify what is deposited in him, thus what you are made of. The God that hides those deposits in the land, hides some virtuous and worth in you. You are made of gold, oil, and the like because you are special to God. You are made in the image of God and you have in you the breathe of God. All that God is made of is in you. Nothing on earth is barren, so you cannot be barren in your dreams of life; you are made to be fruitful in what you do. You are made with values in you. Christ died for you to live, He became poor on the cross for you even without water to drink when He was thirsty so that you would be rich and have it all in Him, and in abundance.

There are some people that are interested in doing what they think others are doing and are successful. There are some youths whose dream is becoming like someone they believed in and trust. But the true question one may ask is "Is that what I am made of?" Your ability is not the same as someone's own; your strength to what you can and can't do might not be the same. What someone does successfully does not necessarily mean that you can also do it and be successful. The only thing that can give you success is your destiny.

Everyone needs to be truthful to him/ herself. You don't love yourself by lying to yourself. You need to be sincere by asking a genuine question, whether what you are doing is actually giving you the fulfillment that you need or not. As a youth, ask yourself if what you are dreaming to do would give you the fulfillment that you need or not. "I always dreamt of becoming a military man when I was a child and almost everyone knew about it because I always talk about it, and with my height, all of them believed that it was a good vision and destiny from God to me. However, when I grew up and began to understand the things of God and could pray for myself, I knew that that is not the plan of God for me, because my motive of going to the military was not the right one and would not benefit me and others, instead it would do harm. This is because the situation and the circumstances around me are calling for revenge in such line of destiny. The environment I was in was the one determining such destiny but not God. Today I am happy to see the leading hand of God on me each day because I am in his plan."

The Bible says God is Spirit, and his worshipers must worship Him in Spirit and in truth. The only way you can worship God in spirit is to be truthful to yourself first and then to God by telling him what you can do and cannot do, your strength and weakness. Paul said in 2 Corinthian 12: 5-9, that he, Paul, would not boast of himself except about his weakness; why? Because he said, the Lord told him that His grace is sufficient for him as his power is made perfect in weakness.

My dear, do not give up on yourself because you are not getting it right, but be faithful and truthful to yourself and tell God all about you and put him to test in his words. Give Him a chance today and He would calm the storm in your life and correct everything. He has your plan in His hand. God loves you, Jesus loves you, and the Holy Spirit is with you to lead and direct you in love to find joy and fulfillment in life. You are blessed, and don't forget that "with God all things are possible".

There are some people who do not like talking about themselves, and there are some who do not even like to think about their own past in order to think about the future even before it comes. I know some people who actually think that talking about their own future, what they want to be, what they want to do and the kind of life they wish to live is not the right thing to do, because it would be a waste of time. Why? Because they are not in that level yet, therefore, they would like to take life in stages, step at a time. But brethren, can I ask you to pause a minute and do some little thinking about yourself? With what you are doing now, can you ask yourself some few questions and give sincere answers to yourself? I might not ask you those questions but you may ask them yourself by reflecting on your life. What happens at work? How do you live your daily life, think about your family and ask, why this? How come? For what reason(s)? What is my fault and what is not my fault? Can I do right or not? By doing this thinking exercise, begin to identify your strength and weakness if possible, and lay them before God…1 Peter 5:7…*Cast all your anxiety on him because he cares for you……Psalm 55:22. Cast your cares on the LORD and he will sustain you; he will never let the righteous be shaken…NIV.*

The grace of God is available to all those who are truthful and faithful to themselves and unto God. Every youth needs to be telling God from now about what interest him or her and keep asking God if that is His plan or if it falls into His plan. Because the will of God is the perfect will for us in everything that we do and wish to do. It is only in His will that we can find the fulfillment we want.

Consider a man who is going to court on a case, of which he wishes to win, but when he went to his lawyer, the lawyer asked him to narrate to him his part of the case, what has really happened and his involvement in the issue, but all that he did was to accuse the other people and keep quiet on his part because he did not believe in talking to anyone about himself. Would such a man win the case in court or loose in court? …..give the answer to yourself.

It is important for us to know that God is a God of freedom; he gives us freedom to make choices, so it's important to let him know about our choice and wishes so that He, as our father can direct us to be winners in all of them to His praise and glory…..*that the name of the Son (Jesus) may give glory to the father.*

Prayer point 1

1. Lord, give me the grace to wait upon your perfect time to give birth to my promise Isaac of destiny.
2. Oh! Lord, open my spiritual eyes and understanding to know the truth about my job and destiny in Jesus name.
3. Anoint me and grant my request to be fruitful and blessed just like it was for Jabesz in Jesus name.
4. Every evil hand holding my star of destiny, cut off by the sword of fire in the name of Jesus.
5. Lord, hold my hand and lead me only in your destiny plan for me that I may find happiness and joy in all that I do and would be doing in Jesus name.
6. Lord, anoint my eyes to see opportunities to my destiny fulfillment in Jesus name.
7. Lord, as it was with Moses, cause the house of any one who is against my destiny to be a blessing to the fulfillment of my destiny in Jesus name.

8. My star, you are anointed to shine, therefore, shine now in the name of Jesus.

9. Thank you LORD for the leadership of the Holy Spirit to the successful destiny fulfillment in Jesus name.

THE REALITIES OF LIFE

> *Psalm 121; I look up to the mountains — does my help come from there? My help comes from the LORD, who made heaven and earth! He will not let you stumble; the one who watches over you will not slumber. Indeed, he who watches over Israel never slumbers or sleeps. The LORD himself watches over you! The LORD stands beside you as your protective shade. The sun will not harm you by day, nor the moon at night. The LORD keeps you from all harm and watches over your life. The LORD keeps watch over you as you come and go, both now and forever. (NLT)*

The grace of God has made it possible for us to identity our destinies by opening our understanding, wisdom and knowledge through His abundant mercy from the beginning of this book. We have known that is only Him that can motivate us to fulfill our special destiny, and by waiting on Him for the appointed time, the abundance of resources deposited in us manifest. When we wait on Him and hold only unto His promise, we shall surely give birth to our

Isaac. In His love, He helped us to understand that when we wait on Him in faithfulness and in truth the devil would not have the opportunity of misleading our destiny plan.

In Him is life, in Him is fulfillment. There are times in our lives that we think God does not care about us and that He is not listening to our prayers. Because some of us, we actually put all hopes on Him for a miracle, for a turnaround in our issues, challenges but it seems our help comes from nowhere. It seems like we are alone. However, He promised to provide us help when we look up to Him ...and my help comes from the Lord ...

The reality of live makes so strong to us sometimes that we think if the Bible is true at all. When the reality of live issues confronted us, we think whether our time and service to God is being rewarded. The Bibles says in 2 Timothy 3:16 (AMP) that, every scripture is God-breathed and given by His inspiration. For the word of God is alive and active. Sharper than any double-edged sword, it penetrates even to dividing soul and spirit, joints and marrow; it judges the thoughts and attitudes of the heart. The reality of live many at times made us question God's words. Sometimes we ask, if the work of God is actually what it is, thus, the breath of God, alive and active, then why my job is not restored, why justices is not giving me, why am I having challenges in my education, why is my investments not working like others, why my financial state is not good though the bible says I shall not borrow but lend to nations, why is the word not active in my life. You are a youth with a lot of dreams and visions, but life is turning you around, misfortunes on your way, is just like nothing is eventually working out good when your hand is in it and you are asking God so many questions. You might be a parent, but it seems like all that you spend your income on is to pay for the hospital bills (either for yourself or children). These are the realities of life. It is important you know that reality of life is real. The question we need to ask ourselves which when answered will determine the answer to many questions we have been asking God is, how am I taking the realities of life that confront me? How am I responding to them? Take a stop and a minute to ask and answer these questions yourself and the truthfulness in your answer would give you the responds to the many questions you have been asking about issues.

The truth about destiny is that it does not always come easy. Every good and great thing must go through serious refinery. However, many at times people truncate their God given destiny due to lack of understanding, and inability to wait on the Lord for perfect manifestation of His glory in their lives. In the book of Job 1, we see how the realities of life unfolded in the face of Job just in a day. He loses all that he had worked for, his seven children died the same day at the same place. What is it that you are going through as a child or youth or even a parent that you can compare to Job's and say yours is more than his? But the Spirit of God recorded for us in verse 22 of Job 1 that, in all of this, Job did not sin by blaming God. He did not charge God for wrongdoing. In fact, in verse 20, the Bible says he felled down upon the ground and worshiped God, thanking Him for all the happenings after he had received the news. Just think of it that is this not too much enough for a man to carry? But in chapter 2 of the book of Job, we could see the conversation that went on between God and Satan for which God made what I called a dangerous pronouncement in verse 6 of which the devil went to afflict Job in verse 7. Job 2: 7 *[So Satan went out from the presence of the LORD and afflicted Job with painful sores from the soles of his feet to the crown of his head. NIV]*. However, in all this he complained but did not charge or curse God for wrongdoing.

Most of us today, even in the Church, even among ministers of God, in our lamentations within periods such as these; we lose control of ourselves and charge God for one wrongdoing or the other. We lose total control of ourselves; we forget who we are in Christ Jesus, some of us either forget about the Bible, prayer or even stop the Church. Some are going to the Church but have given up on their faith and had given themselves to the mercy of the evil wind blowing around them. I don't know who the Lord is talking to, and I don't know which reality of life you have found yourself in, but

God is drawing your attention to Himself today for that miracle you have been expecting. Jesus is saying to you now, if you can focus on Him on the cross by taking your eyes from what you are seeing around, you would receive your breakthrough, you would give testimony of your miracle. *"I prayed into your life that as you come to this understanding and practice it by faith, your testimony would be certain in the name of Jesus. Because he made me know that even with a small faith as small as the mustard seed, I can command mountain to move and it would move.....therefore, in the name of Jesus, I command every mountain that is obstacle on your way to move now....thank you Jesus for the testimony".* The wife of Job and his friends were with him, and in consoling him say all kind of things against God, even the wife told him to curse God and die because God has forsaking him, God has been unfaithful to me but is it true that way eventually no. People cannot be taken out of your life, but God can take them off to have your total concentration to perfect your healing, for Him to perfect that miracle you are expecting that the glory would be for him alone. Job, despite the rejection by the wife and many unkind words of his friends, hold unto God because he know God for himself, he know that his God is too good to have left him alone. Daniel 3:18 *[But even if he does not, we want you to know, Your Majesty, that we will not serve your gods or worship the image of gold you have set up. NIV].* These three Hebrew boys made their stand well known to the King, even when they were faced with the reality of death because they knew that their God can save them; and even if He did not, that does not mean He did not love us, but is for the reason best known to Him.

The captivity of Job was turned around and he was restored in multiple folds after he prayed for his friends [Job 42:10-17]. Shadrach, Meshach, and Abednego, the three Hebrew boys, were attended to by an Angel of God even in the furnace that was heated seven times [Daniel 3:25]. What is it that you are going through and thinking God cannot change it to His glory if you look up to Him as your Lord and savior, and as your only source of hope. Daniel in the book of Daniel chapter 6 was challenged not to pray to his God, but he had total trust and faith in Him to save, hence he prayed to Him alone. With the reality of death, being eating by army of lion, Daniel fear not and he was saved by his God and the king have to made a decree that only the God of Daniel should be served in the land [Daniel 6: 25-27].

The reality of life is real. The reality of life is true, but we need to stop thinking reality and think like sons of God by putting all our hope, trust and faith in Him as our father who is able to save us in whatever we are going through. We should be able to pray to Him, keep focus on Him, His mercy, His loving kindness, His grace for turn around, and for a miracle. The devil would bring people on the way to take your focused attention from God so as to keep you in captivity, but if you can know God for yourselves enough like Job, Daniel, like the Hebrew boys, you can make it. If only you can hold unto Him, your life would be a testimony to others. You are born to rule, you are born to take dominion over the creations of God on earth. Standup now in your faith to take what is yours, pray some more and you would breakthrough. Isaiah 40:31 *[but those who hope in the LORD will renew their strength. They will soar on wings like eagles; they will run and not grow weary, they will walk and not be faint. NIV].* You shall renew your strength in the name of Jesus; you would make it to the higher height, you would soar high like the eagles ...you would rule like kings in the name of Jesus, as you hold onto Him.

The success of life, the greatness in destiny is not built around the realities of life, rather on the word of God. This is because the realities of life always come with the impossibility. The realities of life only point to your weakness instead of the strength you have, what you cannot do instead of what you

> *Romans 7:15 - 20*
> *I do not understand what I do. For what I want to do I do not do, but what I hate I do. And if I do what I do not want to do, I agree that the law is good. As it is, it is no longer I myself who do it, but it is sin living in me. For I know that good itself does not dwell in me, that is, in my sinful nature. For I have the desire to do what is good, but I cannot carry it out. For I do not do the good I want to do, but the evil I do not want to do—this I keep on doing. Now if I do what I do not want to do, it is no longer I who do it, but it is sin living in me that does it. NIV*

can do. Life in the word of God, life by beholding the face of Christ Jesus in total and absolute faith would tell you what you can do, what you are made of, your strength to do instead of weakness. This type of life would tell you and make you understand that it not all about what people around you does or say, rather what God does around you and says about you is all that matters. The truth of what God is doing in our lives, what He is saying about us and what His investments into our lives is and His expectations of us are not found with realities of life, hence, in the face of Jesus-the word of God.

The reality of life is real, but living with the reality of life and believing it would not do you anything good, but harm, distortion, agony and frustration. It would only put you in a total and perpetual bondage by caving you in the camp of the enemy. Why is it so? Is God not with me? Can't God intervene? These and many are the questions that would be going through your mind. Paul says, he wish to do good but does it not, instead the wrong he did not wish to do. That was his reality of life, but the grace of God was available for him because he was determined not to be caged by them but rather to fulfill the call of God over his life. In 2 Corinthians 12: 1- 12, he said he would not boast of himself but rather about his weakness because the Lord told him His grace is sufficient for him and His power is made perfect in weakness. We are being challenged every day by the devil in the face of realities, but if we hold unto God and are determined like Paul, we would also make it to the end. Paul in 2 Timothy 4:7 said he has fought a good fight and have finished the race. In another words, he was saying he had indeed fulfilled to the fullest what he was called for, the destiny of God for him. Jesus said on the cross before He gave up His ghost, that it is finished. In John 17:4, He told the Father, I have brought you glory on earth by finishing the work given Him. Total dependent on God is the only thing that can bring us to a successful end and fulfillment of destiny, but not living, dwelling and meditating on the realities of life and the past we have prayed about many years ago. The reality was there before Paul for everyone to see that he was ones pursuing the lives of those who were preaching the gospel of which he himself have now become an apostle of. The devil would always accuse you by constantly bringing to your remembrance your pass life, telling you lies by confusing you that your sins are not forgiven you, the prayers you pray would not be answered and are not answered because of what you did some times back and that God is still angry with you. All these are tricks that the devil employs to accuse us in our mind, but they are all lies. That does not mean you are not the child of God, no, you are a child of God and the Holy Spirit is with you and will make it difficult for the devil to have access to your heart, therefore, he plays on your mind to rob you of God's blessing as when you are concentrating thinking about those thoughts your attention would be taking away from God. When the devil succeeded in taking your attention from God, then he would bring many deceptive factors to get you totally. He would bring in people that would not say anything good about your God or encourage you to pray, or hold unto God the more, but instead those that would suggest many and multiple demonic ideas to you. They would present them in a nice and genuine ways which in fact would seems to be from God. Many have fallen victim to this trap of the enemy by accepting those deceptions as answered prayer and relaxing at the long run. However, some people were able to detect the devil's scheme and return to God while others still remain with the deception. 1 John 1:19 [*If we confess our sins, he is faithful and just and will forgive us our sins and purify us from all unrighteousness. NIV*]. One thing that you need to know is the fact that the enemy is not necessarily interested in killing you, but deeply interested in taking and frustrating your destiny. Why? It is because every destiny given to man is designed such that when it is fulfilled in God's plan, it gives praise and glory to God while it works against the devil and it agents on earth.

There are more to say under the inspiration of the Holy Spirit, but what I can tell you now is when you hold onto God, He would not disappoint you. God is not a failure and had never failed in anything. He is God; He is too big to bring himself low to fail. Our God never fails and you are not going to be the one He would start failing from. If you hold onto Him, He would honor Himself in your life in that situation. You shall be the head and not the tail in Jesus name.

Today, by the special grace of God I am where I am. If it had been said at my early ages that I will be studying to this level, no one would believed it. Why? Because the reality was so real not to have believed those words even if they were prophesies. I was the last and the thrid born of my mother, and she was the only one taking care of us, hence, I started school when my brother and sister were preparing for their BECE. That was because she had no help from anyone, and out of the proceeds of the little rice she used to sale at the back of our house, she provides for the three of us and herself. You can imagine how real the reality was, but praise be to God that none of us today is wayward, but people that can take and live up to their responsibilities. All is about God and when we are determined to hold onto Him, He would not put us to shame to be mocked by the devil. Micah 7:8 *[Rejoice not over me, O my enemy; when I fall, I shall rise; when I sit in darkness, the LORD will be a light to me. ESV].* We are all who we are today by the grace of God. To those who looked from afar and thought we could not make it, were tight-lipped today seeing our successes. When God is controlling and directing your future, as well as shaping you, you might look laughable to many, but you don't regard them because they do not determine your tomorrow but God.

Your Prophesy Line

Sometimes in life, the quest to understand why the things happening are happening to us will bring us to the knowledge of our destiny line. The prophesies that had actually gone ahead of our birth.

The death and the resurrection of Jesus were long prophesied over 700 years before his birth. The issues that would surround Him as the Messiah were all prophesied by the prophets. [Isaiah 53, Psalm 22, Daniel 9: 24-27], God in His own finance wisdom revealed the destiny plan of the Messiah in prophesy before He was born. This plan that was made public about the Messiah (Jesus of Nazareth, the Son of the living God) was the actual plan revealed in mystery, thus, it was the plan outline that was made known. For that reason, the devil could see and read it but do not know the full details of the fulfillment of the plan. He did not know where Jesus would be at and what would happen at that point in time. Therefore, the devil was taken by surprise by the healing and miracles that Jesus did, even the death of Jesus and His resurrection took him by surprise.

The death of Jesus was the special destiny for which He was born. That special destiny was hiding from the devil by God Himself. Jesus was not born to be an earthly king, so many at times He had to run away from the people because He knew that they wanted to make Him king. It is very important for you to know your special destiny and also to know what the will of God is, in its fulfillment (the manifestation), and also what fulfillment plan He had drawn for its implementation. Why is

> Luke 22:42-44
> "Father, if you are willing, take this cup from me; yet not my will, but yours be done." An angel from heaven appeared to him and strengthened him. And being in anguish, he prayed more earnestly, and his sweat was like drops of blood falling to the ground. NIV

it important for you to know? Because when you know, you will be careful of yourself so as not to be occupied with anything which is not your destiny. There are many people today who are not doing what God has ordained them for, These people are just comfortable, but were not fulfilling their destiny before God.

Jesus would have being occupied with earthly kingship and would not have fulfilled the destiny of reconciling the world to the Father. He was focused on His mission and therefore, always in effective communication with the Father on His destiny line. Did you know your destiny line? How often do you engage God in the discussion of your destiny line or plan? Have you ever in anyway given report of your mission/ destiny fulfillment on earth to God? Have you committed your next phase of movement into His hands for direction, control and protection? In other words, have you ever ask God what His next plan for your life in destiny achievement is and how it is to be fulfilled?

Jesus was in constant communication with the Father about His destiny line. When the reality of death appeared to Him, the flesh was morally down and wanted to give up on the final fulfillment of the plan to man's salvation. However, because He always communicate to the Father on the plan, He gathered the courage and with the faith that the Father would always be there for Him, surrendered the final stage of the plan into the will of the Father, and the Bible says an Angel of the Lord came to strengthen Him. There are many of us today who don't pray anymore, just because we had prayed and fasted but it's like we are seeing no results so we have given up to the mercy of the reality winds. Jesus prayed earnestly and He made it to glory, we can also make it if we look onto Jesus as our hero, the one who have gone through it and succeeded. He knew the glory that awaits Him at the end, so He was determined. If we communicate with God about our line of destiny, we will know at least (if not in full detail) the glory that await us tomorrow which would motivate us to press on. Fear came to Jesus but He quickly come out of it to commit Himself into the will of the Father. It is human to fear because we are living in the flesh, but we don't have to allow the fears of reality take us from God, we must rather live by the application of quick recovery and commitment to God by the demonstration of absolute faith and trust in Him. That will strengthen you to pass through the final phase of reality test to abundant glory.

Jesus has gone through realities of life that came to Him in many ways at different times of His earthly ministration, yet, He made it to His glory. He was successful in destiny fulfillment. All the scriptures and prophesies about Him were fulfilled to the glory of the Father. He is the hero of successful and perfect destiny fulfillment, even in the face of many realities, even the

> Colossians 2:13-15
> ......He stripped all the spiritual tyrants in the universe of their sham authority at the Cross and marched them naked through the streets.MSG

reality of dying on the cross. He made it by giving glory to the Father and brings salvation to the world to the disgrace of the devil by making a public show of him. *Oooh!* Praise God, today we have the Holy Spirit with us (the Spirit of resurrection), we can also make it to glory in destiny fulfillment on earth. Whatever is dead or barren in any part of our lives can receive resurrection and be fruitful if we allow the Holy Spirit to have total control over us.

You have come so far to give up on your awaiting glory. You have waited on God for long a time to now give in to the voice of the enemy. Pray some more, hold on to Him, commit all into His will alone and you would smile at the abundance blessing awaiting you. The prophecy of the Lord over your life has not yet been fulfilled to the fullest, there are more scriptures that needs fulfillment in your life. Submit to the willing power of the Lord today in everything and the frustration plans of the enemy over you would be broken. The Lord promise to frustrate all who frustrate us and bless those who bless us, hold Him on His words in prayer and He would show Himself approve in your destiny achievement. God is the God of His words. You are the next in line for a miracle as you are willing to put God to test in this book.

THE CALL TO JESUS

Mark 10: 46 - 52

Then they came to Jericho. As Jesus and his disciples, together with a large crowd, were leaving the city, a blind man, Bartimaeus (which means "son of Timaeus"), was sitting by the roadside begging. When he heard that it was Jesus of Nazareth, he began to shout, "Jesus, Son of David, have mercy on me! "Many rebuked him and told him to be quiet, but he shouted all the more, "Son of David, have mercy on me!" Jesus stopped and said,"Call him." So they called to the blind man, "Cheer up! On your feet! He's calling you." Throwing his cloak aside, he jumped to his feet and came to Jesus. "What do you want me to do for you?" Jesus asked him. The blind man said, "Rabbi, I want to see." "Go," said Jesus,"your faith has healed you." Immediately he received his sight and followed Jesus along the road. NIV

There are people today that have become comfortable at where they are because of the issues surrounding them. Many have kept quite because they have called on God ones and it looks like nothing happened. I don't know what you might be going through now, but the question is wherever you are and not comfortable, has it become your resting place? Have you taken your blindness in that situation as your permanent condition? The blind Bartimaeus knew that there are people like him that are walking because they can see, hence, he was confident that if others like him can see, then he can see as well. He heard of Jesus and what he was doing, and he believed in Him that He can heal him too. The faith that Bartimaeus had in Jesus worked for him, but he had to put that believe and faith to work first. He could not see, he could not locate the presence of Jesus, but when he heard of Him, he refused to keep quiet for Him to pass by. He shouted even the more when people were rebuking him to be silent. He knew that quietness would not help him and in fact is not about the people but him alone. When Jesus turned, He said, called him. He was healed; he received what his heart had long for.

The reality was that he could not see, and instead of the people around him helping him to get close to Jesus for his miracle, they were rather rebuking him for looking for healing. This is the world we are in. It is a reality that when our time of miracle and breakthrough of launching us into our destiny victory and joy come, people around us will be discouraging us to give up. And many have become victims of this plot of the enemy. Many of us, though we believed and actually have the faith in God, we still remain at where we are in the face of reality, because we are not putting this faith and believe in God to work. This has been and is the challenge to many who have given up and therefore failed in destiny fulfillment. Bartimaeus could have lived and die blind man had he listened to the voice of the people around him. What opportunities do you look for to call Jesus for your healing when you heard that He is passing by? Are you waiting for the voice of the crowd to mute before you call Him or shout even more till He get your attention? Reality is reality, reality would always be a reality of life, but what are you doing to walk away from these negative realities to your glory of freedom. [Luke 19:1-10] Zacchaeus was short and could not see Jesus, but because he was determined, he took advantage of the tree near him and Jesus located him for salvation. [Luke 8: 43-48], when the woman with the issue of blood for twelve years had the believe and the faith that Jesus can healed her, she did not wait for Jesus to locate her among the crowd neither did she wait to see him after everybody had gone, instead, she pushed through the crowd even when people were complaining. She put the faith she was having to actions and was healed.

The limitations that are coming to us today as hindrances to our destiny fulfillment actually have a solution and the solution is a call to Jesus. You might have been praying today but is like your prayers are not producing the needed results and people are looking down on you but you don't need to be quiet because of them but pray more, shout His name the more, push through the crowd till Jesus turn towards you for that breakthrough, even if they are trying to stop you. The Lord is waiting to see our persistence, and our persistence determines if we actually want what we are looking for, and by that we would utilize it well when we receive it. Whoever looks unto Jesus cannot fail no matter what. Jesus is real and still in the business of providing for anyone that seeks help from Him.

IN MY BOAT

Matthew 8:23-37
*Then he got into the boat and his disciples followed him. Suddenly
a furious storm came up on the lake, so that the waves swept
over the boat. But Jesus was sleeping. The disciples went and
woke him, saying, "Lord, save us! We're going to drown!"
He replied, "You of little faith, why are you so afraid?" Then he got up
and rebuked the winds and the waves, and it was completely calm.
The men were amazed and asked, "What kind of man is
this? Even the winds and the waves obey him!" NIV*

I believed God has showed Himself approve by the understanding He has given you from the beginning of this book. God cannot be mocked, whatever a man sows that he reap. The devil is the one in control of the earth, because man gave him the authority through sin. Therefore, he does everything legally right to rob us from the glory that God has ordained for us to rule over the earth. According to God's original plan for us, the earth is to be an extension of the comforts and riches in heaven to live in. Today, many are finding it difficult to make it or succeed in life, because the enemy covers their glory. Even those who made it somehow, could not actually enjoy the blessings of it, because the devil has taken peace away from their lives and homes. The earnings from those successes are always paying hospital bills or some other bills some way with no enjoyment.

There are many that are walking today in different kinds of reality issues that are robbing them from their destiny plan of God and have actually forgotten that Jesus is in their boat. The Lord is always with us, but quiet observing our next steps. The apostles tried what they could but when they knew they could not help themselves, they called unto Jesus, and solution was provided. What reality of life are you facing today? What destiny fulfillment were you robbed of? Jesus is in the boat of your life if only you can call to Him, if only you can be truthful to Him by handing over all to Him. If only you can be open to Him, He would declare solution to you. In fact, every solution has been given by Christ already on the cross, and all that we need is to take the authority in boldness to move forward, to take possession of our right. You see, many at times the devil gets authority over us because of fear. Whenever we conceived fear in our heart in the face of reality, we allowed the devil to take over and destroy our destiny. But the devil in reality is also afraid of us whenever he is trying his attacks, because we have greater authority over him. By the blood of Jesus, we have been restored to the place of glory and authority over the earth.

Dear, Jesus is in your boat. Stand up today as a military man in Christ to dominate what is yours. Reality is real; notwithstanding, you can make it with the Holy Spirit who is with you. You have a great destiny and a promising future; do not give up on yourself; do not give up on your dreams because of what happen today. With Jesus in your boat, you would surely cross over to the other side no matter how heavy and real the storm might be. Jesus is waiting for your call and He would declare permanent solution to the storms and you would forever smile in praise. God loves you and He cares so much about you and has the perfect plan of destiny for you which is awaiting fulfillment. Congratulations to your success!!!!!!

Prayer point II

1. Lord, thank you for opening my eyes to the truth of reality and the way to live with it in destiny fulfillment.
2. Lord, give me the grace to hold unto you, even in the face of reality in Jesus name.
3. I need you to help me fulfill destiny oh! Lord Holy Spirit.
4. Jesus, the son of David, I call you to wake up and save my boat in the storm of reality to make it up to my destiny oh! Lord.
5. Thank you Lord Jesus for being my hero in destiny fulfillment.

Printed in the United States
By Bookmasters